Where Butterflies Grow

by Joanne Ryder · pictures by Lynne Cherry

PUFFIN BOOKS

PUFFIN BOOKS
Published by the Penguin Group
Penguin Putnam Books for Young Readers, 345 Hudson Street,
New York, New York 10014, U.S.A.
Penguin Books Ltd, 27 Wrights Lane, London W8 5TZ, England
Penguin Books Australia Ltd, Ringwood, Victoria, Australia
Penguin Books Canada Ltd, 10 Alcorn Avenue,
Toronto, Ontario, Canada M4V 3B2
Penguin Books (N.Z.) Ltd, 182-190 Wairau Road, Auckland 10, New Zealand
Penguin Books Ltd, Registered Offices: Harmondsworth, Middlesex, England

Library of Congress Catalog Card Number 88-37989
ISBN 0-14-055858-6
Published in the United States by Lodestar Books,
an affiliate of Dutton Children's Books,
a member of Penguin Putnam Inc.
Designer: Riki Levinson
Printed in Hong Kong by South China Printing Co.
First Puffin Unicorn Edition 1996

10 9 8 7 6

Where Butterflies Grow is also available
in hardcover from Lodestar Books.

to my friend Susan Meyers,
who is also delighted by the mystery
and beauty of insects

J.R.

for Bob Karalus, one wonderful friend,
Jo Brewer, a friend to the butterflies,
and the Xerces Society, which is working
to save butterflies and their habitats

L.C.

This is a growing place
green and warm and bright.
Lift up a leaf
and you may find
someone ready to be born.
Lift up a leaf
        and imagine. . . .

Imagine
you are someone small
hidden in a tiny egg
growing bigger
growing darker
till one hot morning
you burst your shell
and creep
into brightness.

Imagine
you are a creeper
thin and dark
living on
a long lacy leaf.
When the wind
tickles the leaf
you and your world
shake.

But you have feet—
two rows of creeper feet
that hold on tight
and keep you safe.

Like a tiny acrobat
you creep,
balancing and
dangling high
above
the earth below.

As you move,
your soft long body
ripples
flowing slowly
along green stems.
You climb up
the stems
to eat the leaves.

As you grow,
you climb
higher and higher
where flowers
spread
like umbrellas.
You nibble and eat
the tiny white flowers.
You eat and eat
till your skin feels tight.

Underneath, you have
a new bigger skin
to grow into.
You swallow air
puffing up and up
till your tight skin splits.

Old and wrinkled,
it falls away
like cast-off clothes.

Look at you now
in a new striped suit!

In this sunny place
you eat and rest
and grow.
But others
are growing too.
You feel one
coming close
and you rear up.
Orange horns
pop
out of your head!
A strong scent
puffs
into the air.
You look so fierce,
the hungry one
darts away,
hoping to find
a better tasting meal.

You grow and grow,
fat and full of flowers,
until one day
you stop
looking for food.

You creep
along the ground
moving as fast as you can,
hunting for some place
tall and firm.
You climb up
a bare, brown branch
and make a silken sling
to rest in.

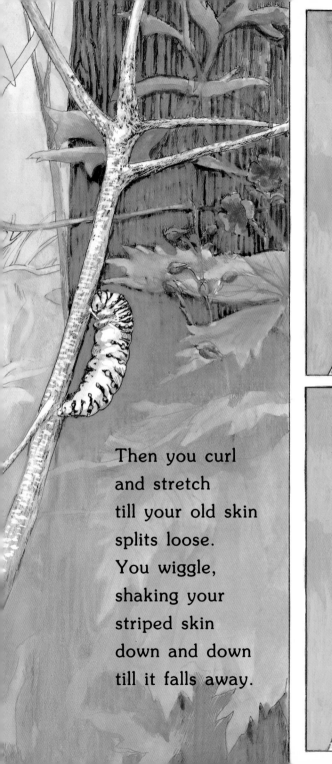

Then you curl
and stretch
till your old skin
splits loose.
You wiggle,
shaking your
striped skin
down and down
till it falls away.

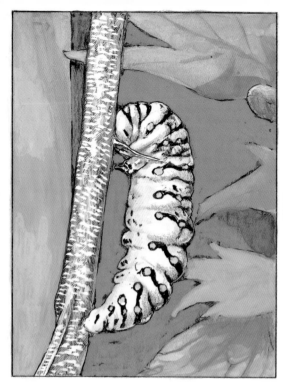

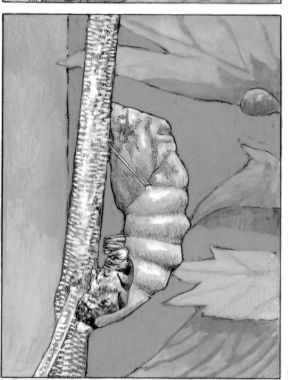

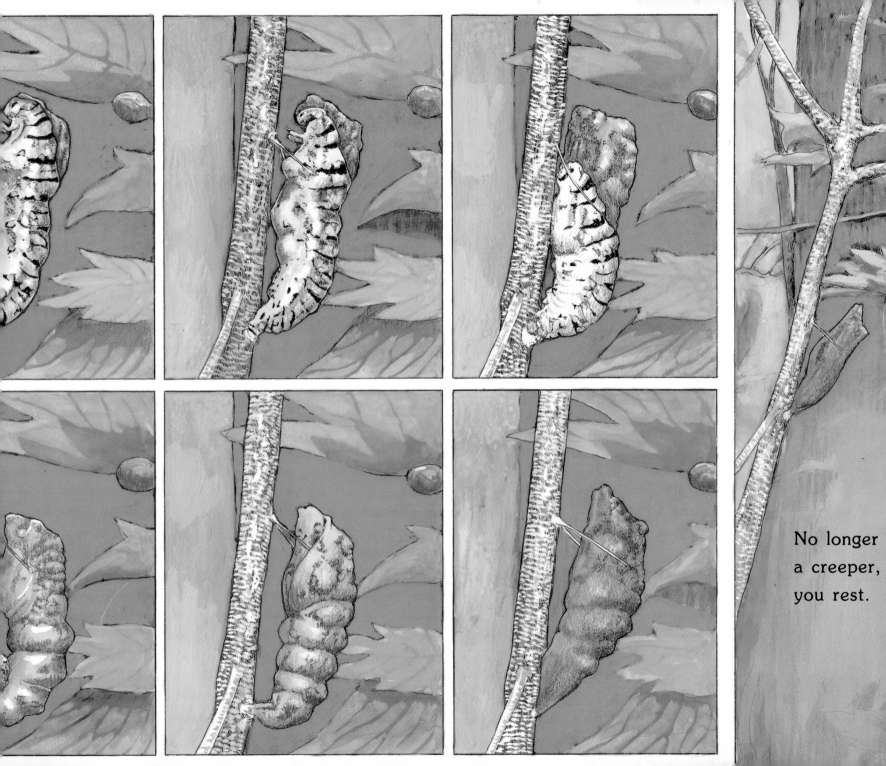

No longer
a creeper,
you rest.

In this green and growing place,
you are hidden, hard to see or find,
resting through the long warm days.
Hungry ones come near
but you are safe,
looking like a small brown twig.

Hidden inside
you are changing,
growing new long legs
growing new wide wings
covered with tiny scales of color.

As you change
you turn darker,
revealing your
black wings
black body
bright yellow spots
all tucked inside.

Until one morning
you are ready
to burst
your twig-like
shell.

You crawl out
wet
crumpled
new.

You dangle high
on long long legs
and hang on tight.
Your four wings
slowly unfold
growing larger
growing brighter
full of bold colors.

You wait,
moving your wings
drying them,
feeling them
grow stronger and harder
till a warm wind
tickles you.

Spreading your wings wide,
you let go . . .
  and fly
   higher and higher.

You drift above the flowers
light and fragile like them.
You touch nothing but sky,
flying far above the ground.

Then you fly low
from bright flower
to bright flower,
landing gently
on the soft petals.
Tasting sweetness
with your feet,
you sip
the sweet nectar
through your
long curled tongue.

You soar
over the bare branch
where you rested,
far above the growing place
where you crept
from leaf to leaf
and flower to flower.
These long summer days
you have grown
and changed
and your world
has grown too.

Now
it's time to fly
to new places,
time to look
for others
like yourself—
bright flyers
in the sun.

Fly, butterfly.
Good-bye.

Growing Butterflies in Your Garden

For as long as I can remember, part of my father's vegetable garden was a garden for butterflies. My father planted parsley—more than our family could ever eat—so that black swallowtail butterflies (*Papilio polyxenes*) would come and lay their golden eggs on the ruffled leaves. When the eggs hatched, we watched the caterpillars grow day by day until they changed into swallowtail butterflies—large, dark flyers with graceful wings shaped like the long tail of a swallow.

You can grow butterflies, too, by choosing certain plants for your garden. Each kind of caterpillar prefers different plants. Black swallowtail caterpillars will eat parsley or carrot leaves, or the leaves and flowers of the common wildflower Queen Anne's lace, as in this book. By growing such plants, you may attract female butterflies to lay their eggs. The tiny black caterpillars that hatch will grow and shed their skin several times, eventually becoming smooth, green caterpillars with black stripes and yellow spots. You may see a young swallowtail caterpillar stick out orange "horns" when disturbed. The horns are tiny pockets that can be pushed out to release a strong-smelling substance that is unappealing to birds and other predators.

To watch a caterpillar grow and change, you can move it carefully to a terrarium with some of its food plant and a stick firmly attached inside. Cover the terrarium securely with a piece of screen or cloth that allows air to enter.

When it is about two inches long, the caterpillar prepares to become a pupa. It stops feeding, and it voids undigested food from its body. It begins to search for a place to pupate. Outdoors, the caterpillar will travel far from its food to some strong, secure place. In the terrarium, it will climb up on the stick or the wall. It attaches itself by spinning a silk pad on a surface and hooking the tip of its body into the pad. It makes a silken sling, then curls up within the sling and rests. In a few hours its skin splits at the head. Underneath, a pale, greenish pupa appears. As the pupa wriggles, the old striped skin continues to split and begins to fall away, until finally it drops to the ground.

As the pupa rests, its surface hardens and changes to a deep green or brown color. Although it looks sturdy, the pupa is rather fragile. Inside, it has already begun to change into a butterfly.

Several days before the butterfly is ready to emerge, the pupa darkens until it appears black. You will see the butterfly's black wings and pale yellow markings underneath. Before the butterfly emerges, it swallows air, puffing up and splitting the pupal shell. It bursts out, wet and crumpled. It swallows more air to pump blood into its wings so they expand, hardening as they dry. At last, the butterfly is ready to be released and take its first flight.

Eggs that are laid early in the summer can develop into butterflies before summer ends. In colder climates, caterpillars born at the end of summer pupate in the fall and do not appear as butterflies until spring. You may keep a pupa indoors through winter. As winter ends, watch and wait until you see the black wings tucked inside the darkening pupa. Soon the swallowtail butterfly will be ready to fly into the warm, green days of spring.